SHAWANGUNK
ROCK CLIMBING

Climbing the thin moves leading to the roof on *Vandals* (5.13)   Mike Freeman

The Shawangunk cliffs

Thunder and Frightening (5.11)   Harvey Arnold

Climbers on *Strawberry Yogurt*. (5.8). Harvey Arnold

SHAWANGUNK ROCK CLIMBING

BY

RICHARD DUMAIS

CHOCKSTONE PRESS

Denver, Colorado
1985

Published by
CHOCKSTONE PRESS
526 Franklin Street
Denver, Colorado 80218

ISBN 0-934641-02-1

Printed by Dai Nippon Printing Company, Japan

LIBRARY OF CONGRESS CATALOGING-IN-PUBLICATION DATA

DuMais, Richard.
    Shawangunk rock climbing.

    Bibliography: p.
    1. Rock climbing—New York (State)—Shawangunk
Mountains—Guide-books.   2. Shawangunk Mountains
(N.Y.)—Description and travel—Guide-books.   I. Title.
GV199.42.N652S533   1985   796.5'223'0974731   85-21256
ISBN 0-934641-02-1

This book is dedicated
to
Fritz Wiessner and Hans Kraus
the pioneers of Shawangunk climbing

Skytop in the Fall.   Mike Freeman

FOREWORD

Hans Kraus and Fritz Wiessner have always told me that the Gunks were already crowded by the time that I arrived in 1951. That may have seemed so, but I remember a gloomy weekend in the Fall of that year when my more experienced friends and I climbed the entire day without seeing another soul until the end of the day, when we met Kraus and his friends.

In the more than thirty years that have passed, one of the most visible changes has been in the sheer numbers of people. Other than the increase in climbers there have been profound changes in climbing and the Gunks has undergone these changes as it has developed into one of the major rock climbing centers in the world. Never would I have dreamed thirty years ago that these quiet cliffs, surrounded as they were in those days by dairy farms, would become a center of intense activity each weekend with climbers, both men and woman, regularly reaching to the standard of 5.12 and beyond.

In those days there was little communication between the various climbing areas in different parts of the world and even in different parts of this country. It wasn't until about 1961 that climbers in the Gunks actually became aware of what was happening in Yosemite Valley. Joe Fitschin's visit began that educational experience. Once contact had been established, the great cross pollination began. Eastern climbers visited the Valley, and the Gunks saw the likes of Yvon Chouinard, Royal Robbins and Layton Kor.

All the while the standards were changing. When I first arrived in 1951, it was widely believed by all the active climbers in the Gunks that the hardest climbs possible were at the level of 5.7. It was known that Wiessner had done a very hard climb, the Minnie Belle, on the Skytop cliff, but little was known about it. First done in 1946, graded 5.8, and rumored to be poorly protected, this hidden gem was unrepeated for so many years that it became almost mythical.

Forced by ignorance to reinvent the wheel, we began in 1957 to explore the mysteries beyond 5.7. This was soon surpassed by a great many individuals, and the grades continued up until they were firmly set at the 5.10 level.

In the late 1960's, John Stannard cracked through to the level of 5.11 and was immediately joined by several others, including Steve Wunsch and John Bragg. Then, in the 1970's, grades reached 5.12, and now are pushing into the 5.13 grade.

Unquestionably, the Gunks is now one of the outstanding rock climbing areas in the world, and for very good reasons. It has outstandingly difficult climbs.

More important, the climbs span every range of difficulty and one does not have to be a master of the extreme to have a safe and enjoyable experience. This special characteristic of the Gunks is not shared by many other rock climbing areas in this country or, for that matter, in the world.

Looking back over the last thirty years, one is struck of course, by the stunning development of skill. 5.7 is no longer the limit of human ability. The climbers of today are only limited by their imagination. And here, more than anywhere, women climbers have come into their own. In an area known for its strenuous climbing, women have excelled and put to rest any notion that they are not capable of leading the most extreme climbs.

And now, 50 years after the first routes were climbed here, Dick DuMais, who has had a lengthy association with the area, has produced this long overdue tribute to Shawangunk climbing.

As a final thought, I would like to remind the climbing community of the enormous debt of gratitude that we owe to the Smiley family for their stewardship of this land. Their foresight in establishing the Mohonk Trust, and later the Mohonk Preserve, combined with their intelligence and good will in maintaining it in such a way that it is open for all activities has been remarkable. Their generous performance in this area is absolutely unequalled.

Jim McCarthy
August, 1985

PREFACE

Despite a rich heritage and enormous popularity, the climbing of the Shawangunks has seen little written about it beyond guide books and the occasional article in climbing magazines and journals. The idea of a book such as this has been considered by numerous individuals during the past decades but has never progressed past the point of initial consideration.

When George Meyers and Merrill Wilson of Chockstone Press approached me about compiling this book, my first reaction was a blend of enthusiasm and apprehension.

Like a great many other climbers, my formative years in the sport had centered around the Gunks and despite the passage of time and various adventures since moving on from there, the memories and effects of that period were still strong. While considering their proposition, I contacted a few other "Gunkies." Their immediate and ebullient response provided the impetus needed to set this project in motion. In the process of compiling information and photographs, the enthusiasm that has been evinced repeatedly by climbers towards the Gunks has been an ongoing source of reassurance.

Needless to say, a project such as this is not possible without the sort of help and encouragement that I have received from a great many people. I would like to extend my heart-felt gratitude to all of you who took the time to assist me, whether with interviews, photographs, information and ideas, or by just listening to my rantings and providing moral support.

Good photographs were absolutely essential to the final product. In the text, credited photographs refer to the contributor, and all uncredited photographs were provided by the author. Following is a list of individuals who have supplied photographs to this work. To each of them I extend a special thanks, for it is these pictures that most effectively convey the many feelings that I know for the Shawangunks.

Rosie Andrews	Rich Perch
Chris Archer	Russ Raffa
Harvey Arnold	Mark Robinson
Russ Clune	Brad Snyder
Mike Freeman	Mark Sonnenfeld
Richard Goldstone	Olaf Sööt
Brian Griffin	Sandy Stewart
Jeff Gruenberg	Hardy Truesdale
Robert B. Hall	Richard Williams
Kim Massie	

The Lost City cliff.

New York would hardly be thought as a big name when it comes to mountain climbing. And yet, less than one hundred miles from New York City is one of the major centers for technical rock climbing in North America. Poised atop the crest of a long ridge west of the town of New Paltz are the steep escarpments of the Shawangunk mountains, which over the years have evolved into a Mecca for East Coast climbers. While the maximum elevation of the range is only 2289 feet, the number of people who frequent these cliffs and the quality and difficulty of the climbs here rivals that of any of the larger and more famous centers of the sport. Because of the firm rock and idyllic setting, and the steep, dramatic nature of the climbing, the Shawangunks are regarded as one of the most appealing rock climbing areas in the world.

Steep climbing on good holds on the exposed arete of *Directissima* (5.9). Rich Goldstone

Autumn leaves along the Overcliff Road.

Various rock outcrops extend along a 7½ mile section of a much longer ridge which dominates the horizon to the west of New Paltz. Most of the land containing these cliffs, and the surrounding terrain was once privately owned by the Smiley family, whose descendants began acquiring it in 1869. After the initial purchase of a small inn and the property near Lake Mohonk the family continued to expand its holdings and built both the Lake Mohonk and Minnewaska Hotels. The Smiley property, eventually extending to 7500 acres, was maintained for the combined purposes of protecting the resort from neighboring development and to assure the preservation of the Shawangunks' unique natural features. In 1903, construction of an elaborate system of trails and carriage roads was initiated; today these provide both extensive hiking opportunities and access to much of the climbing.

Due to the increasing costs of upkeep and management of this enormous tract of land, and to enable it to be maintained in its relatively pristine state, a use fee was instituted in 1958. In 1963 The Mohonk Trust was established, with the goals of furthering education and study as well as the preservation of this land. Gradually the property holdings of this organization expanded to include much of the acreage that was once owned by the Lake Mohonk resort. Shortly after The Mohonk Trust became the Mohonk Preserve in 1981, the area under its stewardship was expanded to over 5000 acres. While a small amount of land immediately surrounding the hotel is still privately owned, the Mohonk Preserve now manages most of the land on which climbing activity occurs. In this manner, the vast majority of the region has been spared from private development and has been kept available for public use.

Tom Scheuer in action. As Senior Ranger of the Mohonk Preserve he has been a familiar face at the cliffs for many years.   Rich Perch

The Shawangunk rock is itself very unusual to the geologist and climber alike. It consists of a horizontally layered quartzite conglomerate, created from sediments deposited on the floor of an immense inland sea which covered· much of the eastern part of the continent during the Silurian period of geologic history (approximately 50 million years ago). After the sediments hardened to rock and were uplifted, the erosion of this formation and of the softer shales underlying it resulted in the east-facing line of cliffs which today dominate the Wallkill Valley below. As layers of rock forming the cliffs have been exposed and eroded, a profusion of cracks and ledges have formed, as well as the myriad overhangs for which Shawangunk climbing is famous.

Due to the steepness and horizontal strata of the cliffs, much of the climbing is of a very "exterior" style—quite strenuous, and often on small face holds or through overhangs. Moving up with only the fingertips and toes in contact with the rock is an airy and exhilarating sensation. When this is combined with the vertical or overhanging nature of many Shawangunk climbs, and with their magnificent exposure, one feels more of an affinity with the air and sky than with the rock itself. Indeed, much that is special about climbing in the Shawangunks is the "feel" of the routes. On many of the easy and moderate climbs, the profusion of good "bucket holds" makes many improbable looking lines possible. Here in the Shawangunks, one can experience the intimidation and commitment common only to far more difficult climbs in other areas.

Support from below. Harvey Arnold

Looking south from Eagle Cliff, along the crest of the Shawangunks.

But along with the rock and the setting, climbing in the Gunks is what it is because of the people. The proximity of the region to an enormous population and the appeal it has as a climbing and recreational area has made it the main climbing center east of the Rockies. As well as serving as a practice ground for those aspiring to greater things, the Shawangunks, since their inception as a climbing area, have been a weekend target for climbers from the Eastern United States and Canada. Over the years, Shawangunk climbers have visited virtually every part of the world. At the same time the Shawangunks have become a crossroads of the climbing world, visited by climbers from all over the U.S. as well as from many other countries.

The climbing history of the region is a story of individuals. Prior to 1935, the area was apparently unknown to climbers. At that time the sport was in its incipient stages in the U.S. and had a very small number of active participants. Most of the emphasis was on mountaineering and the attainment of summits of peaks. The Shawangunks are historically important as one of the first places in the U.S. where rock climbing was actively pursued and where technical advancements occurred.

The second pitch overhang of *Cookie Monster* (5.11)   Mike Freeman

Spectacular and airy climbing on *Carbs and Caffeine (5.10)*.   Russ Raffa

A rainbow over the old Mohonk Gatehouse. Mike Freeman

A strenuous variation to *Three Pines* (5.8). Mike Freeman

Clean and aesthetic moves on *Open Cockpit* (5.11). Sandy Stewart

Fritz Wiessner and the author. Richard Williams   Fritz Wiessner at Skytop.   Richard Williams

Fritz Wiessner essentially opened the Shawangunks to rock climbing. He was a chemist from Germany who, prior to immigrating to the U.S. in 1929 to pursue his studies and business career, had been a leading European climber. In his youth, he started on the sandstone crags near his hometown of Dresden and made many difficult ascents. Always strong and fit, Wiessner was an exceptionally talented climber who exhibited superb technique on rock. European climbing was far ahead of the rest of the world at that time, and Wiessner had already done numerous difficult climbs in both the eastern and western Alps. When he immigrated to the U.S., he brought with him a highly advanced level of climbing expertise. His skill and knowledge of the sport and the numerous important ascents he accomplished thoughout North America set the standards of that era and made major contributions to the development of technical climbing in this country.

As the oft-told story goes, Wiessner was leading a climb on Breakneck Ridge in the spring of 1935. Due to the extreme clarity of air following a thunderstorm, the group was able to see the Shawangunk cliffs far off to the northwest. The next weekend Wiessner and John and Peggy Navas drove north from New York City to explore what they had seen. While the Shawangunks were certainly a major find at the time, the group could hardly have imagined what an important center of climbing this would eventually become.

The first climb, now known as the *Old Route,* was established that day by the three of them on the Millbrook cliff. The following weekend, Wiessner led another exploratory foray to the Trapps. After walking from there to Lake Mohonk, the group put in the *Gargoyle* route on the Skytop Cliff. The very steep and forbidding appearance of this section of rock made for a highly audacious venture. During the next several years, many more routes were established at at Millbrook or Skytop, all led by Wiessner.

In 1939, Fritz met Hans Kraus and soon the pace of Shawangunk climbing accelerated. Kraus was an orthopedic surgeon from Austria. A dedicated physician, he moved to the U.S. in 1938 after an earlier visit when he had been very impressed with the medical advancements seen here. Having also started climbing very young, he had considerable European climbing experience; in the Dolomites of Northern Italy he did many ascents, including great classics of that range. The move to the U.S. had greatly curtailed his climbing career, and when a mutual friend introduced him to Wiessner, it provided an opportunity to resume climbing. Kraus was a powerful climber and possessed a tremendous desire and love for the sport. He was always keen on pioneering new routes, and throughout his climbing career exhibited a flair for picking out lines as well as the drive for pushing many of his bold conceptions to completion.

The facility with which these two men took to climbing in the Shawangunks reflected their considerable experience in climbing on European limestone, most notably in the Dolomites. The physical appearance of the rock of that area bears a striking resemblance to that of the Shawangunks. Likewise, both areas demand steep face climbing. To the two climbers, these relatively small cliffs of superbly sound rock, so similar to the style of climbing that they both relished, were ready-made to their tastes.

Hans Kraus on *High Exposure* (5.6).
Richard Williams

Hans Kraus   Richard Williams

A climber on the crux lower section of *Grey Face* (5.5), one of the earliest climbs in the Shawangunks.   Harvey Arnold

Jackie (5.5)   Brian Griffin

Sound and Fury (5.8)   Brian Griffin

Early hardware: Cassin piton hammer, steel carabiners, and soft iron pitons (left to right) ring blade, angle, wafer, vertical blades, Norton Smithe angle, galvinized Williams angle, small Gerry angle, horizontals, "Ace of Spades," and offset blade.

When Kraus teamed up with Wiessner and others of the small cadre of Shawangunk climbers, the number and scope of the new routes escalated quickly, as did the difficulty of the climbing. Kraus also led climbs, and recalls that during this period he and Wiessner would often take turns putting up new routes with other partners. Then they would come back together and let one another lead the climb.

Still, the future importance of the area was not known to the few climbers of that epoch; they feared that an accident or general lack of interest might terminate the climbing scene there!

In 1941, Kraus began developing routes at the Trapps cliff, the first one being *Northern Pillar.* This was rapidly followed by others, many of them easy and following the most obvious lines, such as *Easy Overhang* and *Southern Pillar.* Through the years these have become traditional beginners' climbs, have been done thousands of times, and are now some of the most frequented routes on the cliffs. During that same year, Wiessner did the first route in the Near Trapps, the *Layback,* so that development of that cliff started as well.

It is ironic that while Millbrook and Skytop were initially and exclusively visited, it is the Trapps that has become THE cliff of the entire area. Originally bypassed as too overgrown to be of interest, this enormous parapet of rock maintains a nearly uniform height of over 200 feet for almost 1½ miles and is the most popular crag in the entire range. The Trapps has now been cleaned by countless ascents and boasts hundreds of routes, many of which are the Shawangunk's best-known climbs.

Steep climbing on *Directississima* (5.10), a super-direct start to the *High Exposure.*
Sandy Stewart

Ending the first pitch on *Horseman* (5.5). This old route is one of the most popular climbs at the Trapps.

Social climbing! Side by side parties in the Belly Roll area of The Trapps.

The Uberfall with a young climber on *Squiggles* (5.4).   Rich Perch

The formation and situation of this outcrop has contributed to the social ambiance of the Gunks. Its proximity to the road and main parking area place it in a central location, and the carriage road along its base not only makes for easy access to the climbing, but enables climbers on the road to spot those on the cliffs and banter back and forth with them. Near the southern end of the Trapps is the Uberfall, the main point of descent from the top of the Trapps and the hub of Shawangunk climbing.

"Uberfall" refers to the original method of descent at this point, when the standard practice was to bridge across, or "fall over," to reach a large detached block and then to scramble down. Here the topography works to funnel the many climbers together. They congregate to recount their recent exploits, meet old friends or find new partners, mingle socially, and refresh themselves at the spring at the base of the descent route. Here, too, is where the outside world comes into contact with the rock climbers, as tourists wander up from the road a short distance below to gape at the weekend hordes on the cliffs. The scene— nearby walls, festooned with ropes and teeming with individuals contorted in airy positions—amazes those unfamiliar with this sport and its subculture. Spectators invariably inquire, "How do you get the rope up there?" or "Are you going all the way to the top?" The atmosphere at the Uberfall characterizes that of the Gunks: friendly and sociable, prone to kibitzing.

34

The next most popular cliff is the Near Trapps which is located just south of the Trapps and across the road. Here a seeming maze of jutting overhangs and a jumble of prows and dihedrals of yellow-colored rock create an immediate and intimidating effect, offering unique climbs.

While the Trapps and the Near Trapps provide the vast majority of the climbing at the Gunks, many other outcrops occur in the range. Immediately south of the Near Trapps is the Bayards cliff, and further south still is Millbrook. This latter crag has a high percentage of difficult climbs, and, at 350 feet, is the highest cliff in the range. To the north of the Trapps is the striking and airy Skytop cliff, and further north still is the scenic Bonticou crag. Scattered throughout the surrounding countryside are numerous small outcrops, often hidden by the dense forests. Of these, Lost City, located due west of the Trapps in the lush Clove Valley, stands out and, despite its modest size, hosts a number of the areas's more noteworthy routes.

The Near Trapps   Rich Perch

The crux section on *Layback* (5.5). This aptly named route was the first climb in the Near Trapps.

The Trapps   Olaf Sööt

The remote and impressive Millbrook crag is the highest cliff in the area. Mike Freeman

Following the initial period of exploration came the World War II years, when as many as 15 to 25 climbers might be present on a weekend. Kraus and Wiessner dominated the area during this time and on through the post-war era, making a great number of first ascents. While those climbs were of a high degree of difficulty for that time, most of them are today considered more moderate. That was the era of the classic climbs, the Golden Age of Shawangunk climbing. Many of the magnificent climbs were created which give the Shawangunks so much of their character and which have become "must routes" for anyone who climbs there. Wiessner made the first ascent of *Yellow Ridge,* with its tricky start and superbly exposed final lead. Kraus put up *Madam Grunnebaum's Wulst,* with its relentlessly steep middle section. And there were countless more as these two men and their small group of friends lived a climbers' dream, putting up new routes at will.

Fritz Wiessner leading the steep middle section of the old Kraus classic, *Madam Grunnebaum's Wulst* (5.6).

Of all these routes, the finest was *High Exposure*. Fittingly, it was first done by Kraus and Wiessner together in 1941. Ascending a prominent buttress, its final pitch features continuously steep climbing on good holds in a magnificent position. At the time it was climbed it was thought so intimidating that over two years passed before any other climbers would lead it. Even today, stepping out onto this final wall is utterly thrilling, and brings home the aptness of the name, "*High Exposure*".

While these two good friends shared a common interest in doing new routes, a stylistic difference began to emerge. Wiessner preferred adherence to free-style climbing, whereas Kraus was more receptive to the potential of aid methods. While an occasional piece of aid had been used for several years, the extensive use of pitons and stirrups for aid first came into play in 1946 when Kraus did the *Hardware Route* at Skytop. He then went on to establish a number of significant routes over the next decade, often utilizing aid techniques. During this same year Wiessner, pursuing free climbs, first climbed the *Minnie Belle*. Graded 5.8 and with little protection, it would for many years be considered the hardest free route in the area.

On a number of Kraus's big climbs of this time he teamed up with Bonnie Prudden. Prudden was a physical fitness specialist who had become involved in climbing. Together they ascended such intimidating lines as *Never Again* and one of the great classics of the area: *Bonnie's Roof*. During the later 1940's and early 50's, Prudden not only established herself as one of the best climbers in the Shawangunks, but also accomplished over 30 first ascents in the area.

Bonnie Prudden belaying using doubled hemp ropes. During her climbing career she made 30 first ascents in the Shawangunks and was one of the leading climbers of that era
Kim Massie

Climbing the final wall on *High Exposure* (5.6). THE classic Shawangunk climb, this pitch was originally led using only three pitons, but now many more are usually in place.

The overhanging first pitch of *Bonnie's Roof* (5.9).   Harvey Arnold

Traversing near the top of *Andrew* (5.4).   Harvey Arnold

By the early 1950's, as many as 60 climbers might show up for a busy weekend at the cliffs. As Wiessner had moved to Vermont this left it to Kraus and Prudden to supply the main impetus for harder climbs. At that time, most of the other climbers were involved in clubs such as the Appalachian Mountain Club (AMC), and the scene was dominated more by bureaucratic and social considerations than by any drive to advance the standards. But this was soon to change.

The Skytop Cliff and Albert K Smiley memorial tower, erected in 1923.

Climbers on the top pitch of *Hans' Yellow Face* (5.6).   Harvey Arnold

The exposed final lead on *Yellow Ridge* (5.7), one of the early routes in the Near Trapps.

Harvey Arnold

A comfortable belay for *Short Climb* (5.10).   Harvey Arnold

Shockley's Ceiling (5.6), the classic Shawangunk overhang.   Robert B. Hall

48

While he was still in prep school, the movie "The White Tower" had kindled Jim McCarthy's interest in mountain climbing. In 1951, as a freshman at Princeton, he first came to the Gunks and then began visiting the area regularly. In 1952 he started climbing with Kraus, under whose tutelage McCarthy rapidly gained knowledge, skill, and experience as a climber. He quickly progressed to the hardest routes and within a very short time assumed the reputation of being the best climber in the area, one that he would maintain for more than a decade.

Early in his career he started doing new routes, the first being *No Glow*, followed by a great many more. Many of these first ascents were with Kraus and were mixed climbs, but by the middle of the 1950's McCarthy started to concentrate on free climbing. With the climbing of *Yellow Belly* in 1957— widely regarded as the area's hardest climb—he initiated a period of intensified difficult climbing in the area. Ten years later, in 1967, he and Richard Goldstone made the first free ascents of *Try Again* and *Coexistence*, which had the same catalytic effect on the climbing scene. In the interim he did over sixty new routes and methodically eliminated the aid from many others. When he free climbed *Retribution* in 1961, it brought the 5.10 level to the Shawangunks, and this was soon followed by other equally difficult feats. In 1964, when the first guide book was published, McCarthy was credited with every free route listed at this top grade.

Jim McCarthy   Richard Williams

McCarthy traveled widely and was instrumental in introducing international concepts, standards, and climbers to the Gunks. Competitive by nature, he worked hard, despite the demands of his law practice, to maintain his high level of climbing and his role as preeminent climber in the eastern U.S. He thoroughly enjoyed difficult routes and thrived on the challenge and thrill that they afforded. Today a common thread connects any of the routes with which his name is associated: whatever their length, style, character, or grade, they are invariably hard. For nearly fifteen years McCarthy and his routes constituted the Shawangunk standard by which all the leading climbers were measured, and historically he stands out as one of the most important figures in Shawangunk climbing.

Early footgear: (left to right) The Solda boot, Spider and Kronhoffer kletterschues

Climbers on the second pitch of *Grand Central* (5.9).

Richard Goldstone

Traversing along the roof on the first pitch of *Matinée* (5.10).   Harvey Arnold

The initial traverse on *Disneyland* (5.6). Richard Williams

But McCarthy was not alone at the top during this period of accelerating difficuty. There had been an increase in the number of climbers at the Gunks, many of whom were keeping up with these new standards. The most noteworthy of these was Art Gran, whose interest in hiking and the outdoors had led him into climbing while he was a student at Cooper Union. Gran did not have the advantage of learning the sport from an accomplished mentor; slowly and methodically he worked his own way up the scale. Accompanied only by a small group of CCNY students and detached from the mainstream climbing community, many of his accomplishments were initially overlooked.

By the mid 1950's, however, Gran had emerged as one of the key figures in the climbing scene at the Shawangunks and had become McCarthy's leading competitor for the position of the area's top climber. This intensified the extent to which both men pushed themselves, and this in turn accelerated the development of the climbing, eventually bringing the two men together as partners on many new routes.

In 1960, Gran, accompanied by Dave Craft and McCarthy, made the first ascent of *Never Never Land*. At the time, this route had a short bit of aid but was still the first climb in the area to be graded 5.9. Soon after this, McCarthy did another 5.9 route, *M.F.*, a climb that has become one of the classics of the Shawangunks. This move into a more difficult level opened up the possibility of many new lines, and these two men quickly amassed a large number of top level ascents during the next few years.

Art Gran   Richard Williams

Twilight Zone (5.4 A2) climbs through an enormous roof. First done by Gran in 1964, it is one of the few remaining aid climbs in the Shawangunks.   Brad Snyder

The first pitch on *Never Never Land* (5.10).

Fritz Wiessner on *Never Never Land* (5.10) in 1973.

An early Vulgarian crew. Richard Williams

But even more than the climbs of the period, the late 1950's and early 60's produced a phenomena that has earned the Shawangunks a lasting notoriety: the Vulgarians. This group came into being when a few independent local climbers, most notably Dave Craft, began to team up with Claude Suhl and others of the CCNY group. It's difficult for today's climbers to imagine the situation that existed at that time. Prior to the arrival of the Vulgarians, the clubs, especially the AMC, exerted a tremendous amount of influence on the Shawangunk climbing scene, including some very bureaucratic elements. This influence was so restrictive, even reaching the point of trying to delegate who could lead or follow climbs, that it was effectively stifling the development of climbing and had alienated most of the better climbers.

The influx of young climbers who were eager to push themselves and who disdained the traditionalism of the existing establishment resulted in a sizeable schism between the two factions. With the enthusiasm and rebelliousness of youth, the Vulgarians' refusal to comply with the accepted procedures had an immediate effect. Berating the Vulgarians for "loud and ungentlemanly behavior," the reaction of the club faction was to attempt to increase restrictions, which only encouraged increasingly outrageous responses. An attempt to close the cliffs to "non-certified" climbers by some "Appies" met with little success, but did lead to a series of confrontations. On one occasion a group of Appies leaving a local bar were showered from the roof of the establishment by Vulgarian urine. Another incident saw zealous Vulgarians overturn the car of an exceptionally objectionable antagonist—only to learn that they had vandalized the wrong vehicle!

Another highlight of this era was the Vulgarian Grand Prix. This was a free-for-all car race on back roads around the cliffs and was often won by whomever managed to grab the lead and then obstruct traffic sufficiently to prevent others from passing. In later years the glamour of the group was greatly enhanced by Joe Kelsey's publication of *The Vulgarian Digest*, which satirized the national and local climbing scenes. Visits by the Vulgarians to Western climbing areas extended their raucous presence and reputation across the country, often to mixed reception.

The factual basis of many of their escapades has been distorted by retelling or has faded with time, until it becomes difficult to tell what really occurred. Were they semi-mythical heros of the climbing community, akin to Robin Hood and Rasputin? Or were they simply, as one disgruntled climber put it, "that bunch of jerks that kept me up all night in the Tetons, screaming and banging on garbage cans?" Whatever the case, their spirit of free-living rebellion caught the fancy of later generations, and tales of Vulgarian exploits have gained a lasting place in the lore of Shawangunk climbing.

Dave Craft   Richard Williams

The strenuous crux overhang on *Retribution*, the first 5.10 in the Shawangunks.
Harvey Arnold

The free ascent of *Coexistence* (5.10) in 1967 heralded a new
period of rising free climbing standards.   Rich Perch

The period of the late 1950's and early 60's saw another development. Whereas the Shawangunks had originally been a relatively insular area, not widely visited except by Eastern climbers, it began evolving into a more major and far-reaching climbing center. Visitors from the Western U.S., and from other countries, as well, began to arrive with increasing frequency. In 1964, Art Gran's guide book, *A Climbers Guide to the Shawangunks,* was published, and still more climbers began flocking to the area. Interaction with other areas led to the inclusion of many of their ideas and technical advancements, and with McCarthy's free ascents of *Retribution, Never Never Land,* and *Matinée,* the 5.10 level had become firmly established at the Gunks.

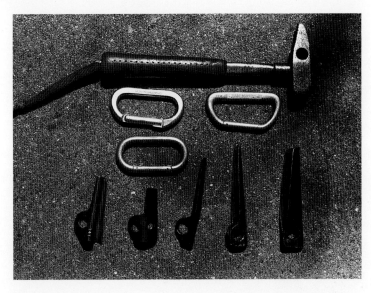

A CMI piton hammer, aluminum carabiners, and chrom-moly pitons (right to left) Chouinard angles, Lost Arrow blade, knifeblade, Leeper Z.

By the late 1950's, another young climber had begun to establish his presence among the ranks of the area's leading figures. Dick Williams had been a competitive gymnast in high school, and once he started climbing in 1957, while in the Navy, he took to the sport with gusto. After leaving the service, he climbed on a regular basis and was soon doing the hardest routes. Williams' climbing style was uniquely dynamic, perfectly suited to the steep rock of the Shawangunks, and he was considered by many of his contemporaries as the finest and most naturally talented climber that the area had yet produced.

Williams seemed driven to do first ascents. He teamed up with McCarthy, Craft, Gran and other top climbers of that period, and over the next few years produced a prodigious number of new routes. As well as his many free routes, he enjoyed aid, and some of his best efforts involved difficult mixed climbs like the *Yellow Wall* and *Fat City.*

The top section of *Arrow* (5.8).   Harvey Arnold

Dick Williams

As the 1960's progressed, a temporary lull set in. The original climbers had slacked off their activity, many of them moving on to other interests. The 50's generation was moving on as well, and even the Vulgarians were beginning to approach middle age. But once again new faces began to appear, along with other factors which would precipitate the next surge of activity.

John Hudson and Kevin Bein were young climbers who both appeared on the scene early in the 1960's. Hudson possessed tremendous climbing talent, but his self-effacing nature often glossed over the high level of his accomplishments. A frequent climbing partner of both Gran and Williams, he accomplished many difficult ascents in a short but impressive career. Sadly, before his full potential could be realized, he died while climbing in South America.

64

A climbing party high on *Sound and Fury* (5.8).   Harvey Arnold

The Yellow Wall (5.11) wends its way up the most spectacularly overhanging section of the Trapps.   Mike Freeman

The last pitch of *Yellow Wall* (5.11)   Brian Griffin

Although young and perhaps lacking Hudson's natural skill, Bein was dedicated to the sport, and through extensive gymnastic training, bouldering, and hours at the cliffs, he steadily progressed to doing very difficult climbs. In 1966, thinking he was climbing *M.F.*, he free climbed *Birdie Party*, a very hard ascent for that time. Just as he was coming into his own, a serious fall interupted his climbing career. Although he eventually recovered and has always continued to climb at a very high level, this kept him from participating in the very active period that occurred during the late 1960's, during which he would certainly have been a key figure.

During the mid 1960's a young mathematician named Richard Goldstone began climbing regularly in the Gunks. Early in his climbing he had encountered the legendary John Gill, who had exerted a tremendous influence on Goldstone's attitudes toward the sport. Through Gill he became acquainted with smooth-soled climbing shoes, chalk, and the concept of gymnastic training and extensive bouldering to develop free climbing skills. He brought these innovations with him when he came to the Shawangunks and provided fresh energy to the upper echelons of the local climbing community. In 1967, when he and McCarthy free climbed *Try Again* and *Coexistence*, it sparked the next surge of interest in pushing hard climbing.

Kevin Bein   Harvey Arnold

Richard Goldstone   Richard Goldstone

68

A steep corner on *Son of Easy-O* (5.8).   Chris Archer

The first pitch on *Fat Stick* (5.7) displays the unique nature of Near Trapps climbing.
Rich Perch

Swinging free near the top of *Modern Times* (5.8)   Hardy Truesdale

At this time there were major changes in the sport of rock climbing going on throughout the world. The overall focus of the sport was beginning to shift, and tremendous advancements in equipment were beginning to occur. Until the early 1950's, the gear had been primitive. Double hemp ropes had caused severe problems with weight and drag, while steel carabiners and soft steel pitons of a very limited selection had been the extent of the hardware available. Gym shoes had normally been used for footgear.

Kraus had introduced very stiff, lightweight leather boots called "Soldas" in the late 1940's, and they had become the locally accepted shoe. In the early 1950's, Weissner introduced nylon ropes, which were better than hemp, and aluminum alloy carabiners started to become more commonplace as European gear gradually filtered into the American climbing scene. These advances contributed greatly to the progress of climbing in the 50's, but the gear was still cumbersome and failed to contribute much to confidence or security.

Left to right: the RD, one of the early smooth-soled shoes; the RR Yosemite; and the Vasque Ascender. All three shoes were popular in the late 1960's and early 70's.

By the late 1950's, European *kletterschue* were becoming more commonplace and replacing the Solda boots. These light, tight-fitting shoes encouraged increasingly difficult levels of climbing during the next several years. Perlon *kernmantle* ropes were first brought to the area by Kraus in the late 1950's, and, because their improved handling made climbing far less tedious, they caught on quickly. And most importantly, the advent of chrom-moly pitons in the early 1960's brought a new measure of security and greatly expanded the possibilities for protecting routes.

72

Following the steep first pitch of *Pas de Deux* (5.7).

Gravity's Rainbow (5.12) is one of the fine, hard routes on the Lost City cliff.   Sandy Stewart

Trinity (5.11)   Mike Freeman

But it was in the second half of the 60's that really major changes appeared. The advent of smooth-soled shoes made specifically for rock climbing was a significant improvement. Training and bouldering was introduced, and became an accepted practice rather than a rarity practiced by a few. The use of chalk also began on a limited scale, occasionally for bouldering or at the crux of a very difficult climb. But by the end of the decade, its use had become widespread on climbs of all levels, and it was considered mandatory for many climbs.

Changes in protection hardware have been even more dramatic. The use of nuts (artificial chocks) was greeted with initial skepticism. They were promoted as causing far less damage to the rock than pitons, but the ease of placement and removal and the greater range of use soon became apparent as well. Being far less tiring to place, their innovation has contributed significantly to the raising of free climbing standards. In more recent years, further refinements such as very small, wired chocks and the development of mechanical devices like Friends have continued to improve and expand protection potential, and to be instrumental in opening up many of the new, extremely difficult modern climbs.

A variety of chocks: (left to right) Hexes, Moac, and Stoppers. The use of nuts has contributed greatly to the rise in standards of difficulty.

Fall foliage reflected in the Coxing Kill.

John Stannard Russ Raffa

In the latter part of the 1960's, the emphasis in rock climbing began to shift markedly. The sport was no longer regarded as merely training for mountaineering, but as an end in its own right. The orientation toward very difficult and often short free climbs was perfectly suited for the Shawangunks. Not surprisingly, climbers adapted rapidly and began again to push forward the levels of difficulty.

Foremost among this new generation was John Stannard, a physicist who lived in Maryland and climbed at the Shawangunks on weekends. He was physically well-suited to climbing, being slightly built and very agile. Stannard possessed an incredible degree of dedication to the sport, and a persistence at attacking problems and at ultimately succeeding where others might not. At home and at work he did exercises and even designed mechanical devices to develop his strength for specific problems.

When he managed to free climb the huge overhang on *Foops* in 1970, it was not only considered to be far harder than any existing problem, but also to be a significant advance in free climbing in the entire country. This feat led to a serious reconsideration of the possibilities for Shawangunk climbing.

Stannard continued to advance standards with his ascent of *Persistent*. Accomplished in 1971, this was the first 5.11 climb in the area (*Foops* was graded 5.10 at that time), and represented another big breakthrough. But as important as his climbs has been his effect on climbing ethics. His dedication to preserving the area, to climbing routes "clean" and not resorting to bolting, had a profound effect on the ethical considerations and attitudes that persists in the Shawangunks today.

John Stannard on *Foops* (5.11).

Persistent was the first climb in the Shawangunks to be graded 5.11.   Rosie Andrews

Persistent (5.11) Mike Freeman

Happiness is a 110° Wall (5.12) derived its name from how the first ascent party felt when this pitch finally leaned back to that angle. Mark Robinson

Small wired nuts and Friends have revolutionized protection.

The Throne (5.11). Rosie Andrews

The Coxing Creek in the Clove Valley.   Robert B. Hall

No Exit (5.10).   Harvey Arnold

Steve Wunsch Harvey Arnold   John Bragg Mark Robinson

In a very short time, more new young climbers appeared on the scene, repeating these routes and doing numerous other ascents of equal and greater difficulty. In 1973, John Bragg free climbed the enormous ceiling on *Kansas City*; this was graded 5.12. Then, in 1974, Steve Wunsch did the *Super Crack*.

Wunsch was a full-time climber who travelled from one rock climbing center to the next all year long, following the seasons. He was well-known for his extremely difficult climbs in virtually every principal rock climbing area, and his strict adherence to free climbing ethics had earned him the title "the prophet of purism." Located on a small outcrop near Skytop, the striking one inch crack that he climbed brought Shawangunk climbing into national prominence once again. *Super Crack* was originally graded 5.13 and was the first route of that grade in the U.S. Subsequently it has been down-graded to 5.12, but an ascent of *Super Crack* is still highly prized by free climbing afficionados.

The relentlessly steep and difficult *Super Crack* (5.12). Harvey Arnold

Following the ascent of *Super Crack*, the number of new routes again increased dramatically as the possibility for new lines expanded with the rising standards. Throughout the 1970's the new route activity was primarily affected by the emerging generation of climbers. After Wunsch entered the world of business and cut back on his climbing, it was John Bragg who dominated top-level activity for the next few years, though by the end of the decade Rich Romano was taking over as the leading figure. Commendably, Romano shunned the publicity that so often accompanies this position. He concentrated his efforts on new routes at lesser-known and more remote areas, especially the Millbrook cliff, where during the late 1970's and early 80's he systematically exhausted most of the possibilities of that outcrop and in the process created a legacy of hard climbing. His routes of great difficulty with minimal protection exhibited a degree of seriousness and commitment, serving as a forerunner to the next generation of climbs.

Moving across the huge ceiling on *Kansas City* (5.12).   Mark Robinson

Making a long reach at the start of *Scare-City* (5.10).   Sandy Stewart

Finishing a wildly overhanging section of *Fat City* (5.10)   Mark Sonnenfeld

Skytop and Lake Mohonk Olaf Sööt

As the climbing moved into the 80's, this trend toward routes of extreme difficulty and with minimal protection has continued. In 1981, Hugh Herr did *Sticky Bun Power*; the difficulty of the newer routes had clearly surpassed the standards established by the ascent of *Super Crack*. Russ Raffa, another outstanding local climber from the 70's generation, kept pace with Herr, establishing many of his own climbs of a comparable level. These two joined with Lynn Hill, Jeff Gruenberg and others of a growing group of top-rank climbers seeking to further the degree of difficulty toward the 5.13 level. This was finally achieved in 1983 when Gruenberg, Herr, Hill and Russ Clune managed, in a prolonged team effort, to complete *Vandals.*

Hugh Herr   Russ Clune

Rich Romano   Sandy Stewart

92

Starting the imposing roof on *Swing Time* (5.11).   Russ Clune

Russ Raffa   Harvey Arnold

Lynn Hill   Russ Raffa

Jeff Gruenberg   Russ Clune

Testing the "Pancake" on *Nectar Vector* (5.12)   Mike Freeman

The very difficult *Sticky Bun Power (5.12)*.   Mike Freeman

The crux roof on *Vandals* (5.13).   Russ Raffa

Talus Food (5.11), a very serious and difficult lead.   Mike Freeman

Crash and Burn (5.9) starts with this exciting move.   Mark Robinson

When the 1972 edition of *Shawangunk Rock Climbs*, by Dick Williams, was published, there was no doubt but that the Shawangunks was already well-established as a leading center of rock climbing. In addition to the many climbers who visited the area from elsewhere, a permanent population of enthusiasts had taken up residence in the surrounding region, and New Paltz was boasting its own climbing shop. While Gran's original 1964 guide book had listed 290 routes, that number had increased to almost 400 in 1972. By the time the second edition of Williams' book was published in 1980, this number had grown to well over 500. Only one year later, an updating publication, *Shawangunk Grit*, saw the number near 700, and by the time a 1984 supplement appeared, there were nearly 1,000 known routes plus uncounted variations.

A fiercely overhanging section on *Tiers of Fear* (5.12).   Russ Clune

Attempting to rest on *Nectar Vector* (5.12).   Mike Freeman

It is worth noting that throughout this development the Shawangunk climbers have shown a strong reluctance to compromise the rock for the sake of executing advancements. Unlike some other areas where bolts have proliferated as a means of opening new routes or advancing the standards of difficulty, this has not been the case in the Gunks. This is largely due to the legacy established by John Stannard. Many of the top figures of his era and of the period which followed came directly or indirectly in contact, early in their climbing careers, with Stannard or with the purist ethics of Wunsch. As time has passed, the effect of this early contact has been to establish an attitude and tradition which have continued through the years. Looking to the future of Shawangunk climbing, one hopes that this desire to preserve the natural and adventurous qualities of the climbing will persist and not be compromised.

Starting the traverse on *Thin Slabs Direct* (5.8).

A climber on *No Exit (5.10)*.   Mike Freeman

Birdland (5.9), one of the finest of the "Land" climbs.   Chris Archer

Passing the overhang of *Half Assid* (5.10).   Mike Freeman

Throughout the history of Shawangunk climbing, another tradition has been the imaginative naming of the climbs. In other areas, especially in their early history, route names have been basically of a descriptive nature (*North Buttress, East Ridge*) or have been named after the first climbers (*Steck-Salathé, Durrance Ridge*). While some Shawangunk routes, such as *Northern Pillar* or *Shockley's Ceiling*, fall into this category, many others, such as *Inverted Layback* or *High Exposure*, evoke the character of the climb.

In the realm of the pun, nuance, and innuendo, the names of Shawangunk climbs have excelled, a practice which ultimately spread to other areas. *High Exposure* was followed by *Rear Exposure*, and, inevitably, *Indecent Exposure*. There is a whole series of "land" climbs—*Disneyland, Wonderland, Birdland, Never Never Land, Absurdland,* and, finally, *Land's End.* Then there are such tongue-in-cheek names as *Kligfield's Follies, Climb and Punishment,* or *Gorilla My Dreams.* Many routes are named in series, after songs, movies, literary references, bizarre events, or flights of fancy that crossed the first ascent party's collective mind. *Bitchy Virgin, Son of a Bitchy Virgin, Something Interesting, Something Boring, Farewell to Arms, Lito and the Swan, City Lights, Modern Times, Kansas City, Akidleativytoowouldn'tyou, Cascading Crystal Kaleidescope, Erect Direction,* and *Falling Monkeys Gather No Moss* are just a few examples. Indeed, reading through the list of climbs in the guidebook is an entertaining exercise.

EB's and Fire's—popular modern shoes.

Climbers on the *Flashdance* (5.11) arete.   Jeff Gruenberg

Strenuous moves on *Kligfield's Follies* (5.11).   Russ Clune

The thin start to *Mystery Woman* (5.10).   Mike Freeman

A splash of Autumn color along the Undercliff road.

Persistent (5.11)   Mike Freeman

Belaying the top pitch of *High Exposure* (5.6)   Rich Perch

Stretching for a handhold on *The Sting* (5.11).   Russ Clune

The unique climbing experiences that one encounters in the Shawangunks create their own special memories and impressions. Foremost among these has always been the extraordinary beauty of the Shawangunk Range and the setting of the cliffs. The exciting style of the climbing and the conviviality of Shawangunk climbers are also significant. Finally, there is the aura of climbing history and heritage missing in many other climbing areas.

While every Shawangunk climber has personal feelings for the area, Fritz Wiessner's comment over 25 years ago may speak for all:

"It is rare in our day of over-exploitation of the land to find, near to a large city, country which is still unspoiled by man and as beautiful as when it was created."

The final moves on *Scare-City* (5.10). Harvey Arnold

BIBLIOGRAPHY

Appalachia: June, 1960

Climbing: Issues #10, 14, 18, 54, 73, and 83

Gran, Arthur: *A Climbers Guide to the Shawangunks,* Published by the
American Alpine Club, N.Y.C., 1964

Jones, Chris: *Climbing in North America,* Published by the University of
California Press, Berkeley, 1976

Morrisey, Thomas: *20 American Peaks and Crags,* published by Contemporary
Books, Inc., Chicago, 1978

Mountain: Issues #21, 73, 97

North American Climber: July, 1975; November, 1975; Winter, 1977

Off Belay: Issue #43

Rezucha, Ivan: *Shawangunk Grit,* Privately published, 1981, 1984

Williams, Richard: *Shawangunk Rock Climbs,* Published by the American
Alpine Club, N.Y.C., 1972, 2nd edition 1980

Vulgarian Digest: Privately published, Issues #1, 2, 3

Winter at the Lake Mohonk Hotel.   Olaf Sööt